M000288146

United States Presidents

George Bush

Paul Joseph
ABDO Publishing Company

visit us at
www.abdopub.com

Published by Abdo Publishing Company 4940 Viking Drive, Edina, Minnesota 55435.
Copyright © 1999 by Abdo Consulting Group, Inc. International copyrights reserved in
all countries. No part of this book may be reproduced in any form without written
permission from the publisher.

Printed in the United States.

Cover and interior photo credits: AP/Wide World, Archive, Corbis-Bettmann

Contributing editors: Robert Italia, Tamara L. Britton, K. M. Brielmaier
Book design/maps: Patrick Laurel

Library of Congress Cataloging-in-Publication Data

Joseph, Paul, 1970-
    George Bush / Paul Joseph.
        p.   cm. -- (United States presidents)
    Includes index.
    Summary: Surveys the childhood, education, military career, and political life
of the forty-first president of the United States.
    ISBN 1-56239-816-4
    1. Bush, George, 1924- --Juvenile literature. 2. Presidents--United States--
Biography--Juvenile literature. [1. Bush, George, 1924- . 2. Presidents.] I.
Title. II. Series: United States presidents (Edina, Minn.)
E882.J67 1999
973.928'092
[B]--DC21
                                                                97-53066
                                                                    CIP
                                                                    AC

Second printing 2002

Contents

George Bush

*G*eorge Bush has achieved much in his life. During **World War II**, he was the youngest bomber pilot in the U.S. Navy. He received four medals for bravery.

After the war, Bush entered Yale University. He graduated with honors in less than three years. In 1948, Bush moved to Texas. There, he succeeded in the oil business.

In the 1960s, Bush became a politician. He entered the U.S. **Congress** in 1966. In 1970, he was the U.S. **ambassador** to the **United Nations**. In 1973, Bush led the **Republican National Committee**.

In 1974, Bush became the first U.S. **envoy** to the People's Republic of China. By 1976, Bush led the **Central Intelligence Agency (CIA)**.

George Bush

4

In 1980, Bush wanted to run for president. But the **Republicans** chose Ronald Reagan. He asked Bush to be his vice president. Reagan and Bush won the election. They were re-elected in 1984.

Bush was elected U.S. president in 1988. He helped reduce the number of nuclear weapons in the world. He led the war against drugs. And he earned praise for his leadership during the Persian Gulf War.

Bush's journey to the White House began many years earlier in a town outside of Boston, Massachusetts.

President Bush (center) poses with his family in the White House.

George Bush (1924–)
Forty-first President

BORN:	June 12, 1924
PLACE OF BIRTH:	Milton, Massachusetts
ANCESTRY:	English
FATHER:	Prescott Sheldon Bush (1895-1972)
MOTHER:	Dorothy Walker Bush (1901–)
WIFE:	Barbara Pierce (1925–)
CHILDREN:	Six: 4 boys, 2 girls
EDUCATION:	Phillips Academy, Yale University
RELIGION:	Episcopalian
OCCUPATION:	Businessman
MILITARY SERVICE:	Lieutenant, U.S. Navy (1942-1945)
POLITICAL PARTY:	Republican

OFFICES HELD:	Ambassador to the United Nations; head of the Republican National Committee; U.S. envoy to the People's Republic of China; director of the Central Intelligence Agency (C.I.A.); vice president
AGE AT INAUGURATION:	64
YEARS SERVED:	1989-1993
VICE PRESIDENT:	J. Danforth "Dan" Quayle

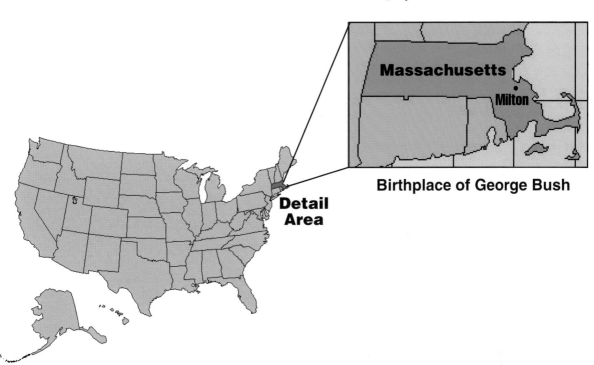

Massachusetts

Milton

Birthplace of George Bush

Detail Area

Young Poppy

*G*eorge Herbert Walker Bush was born June 12, 1924, in Milton, Massachusetts. His parents were Prescott and Dorothy Bush. George was the second of five children.

George as an infant

George's mother named him after her father, George Herbert Walker. She called her father Pop. So, young George became Poppy. The nickname stuck for many years.

When George was a year old, the family moved to Greenwich, Connecticut. The house had six bedrooms and a large playroom. The Bush family had maids, a cook, and gardeners.

The Bush children were disciplined, well behaved, and generous. George often shared his toys, treats, and snacks. His friends and family sometimes called him Have Half.

The Bush family was very close. They spent their summers on the Maine coast at Kennebunkport. Here, a **peninsula** called

Walker's Point reaches into the Atlantic Ocean. Dorothy Bush's father and grandfather bought the **peninsula** in 1899. The Bush children went fishing, swimming, and sailing.

George attended private schools. First, he went to Greenwich Country Day School. Then George attended the Phillips Academy in Andover, Massachusetts.

George was an excellent student. He was the captain of the basketball and soccer teams. He also played for the baseball team. As a senior, George was voted class president.

George Bush with his youngest brother, Bucky, in 1942

Navy and Yale

*A*merica entered **World War II** in 1941. Bush graduated from Phillips Academy in 1942. Then he joined the U.S. Navy. He finished his flight training at the Naval Air Station in Corpus Christi, Texas. Now, he was a navy officer.

In 1943, Bush was sent to the aircraft carrier USS *San Jacinto*. At 19, he was the youngest navy pilot.

Bush had many dangerous flights during the war. He was shot down off the coast of Japan on September 2, 1944. He was soon rescued. Bush received four medals for bravery while in the navy.

Bush returned to America to train navy pilots. On January 6, 1945, he married Barbara Pierce. She attended Smith College. Her father published the magazines *Redbook* and *McCall's*.

Bush as a navy pilot

In September 1945, Bush left the navy. He entered Yale University. There, he studied economics and played baseball.

In 1946, George and Barbara had their first child, George W. Bush. Robin was born in 1950. John, known as Jeb, was born in 1953. Neil was born in 1955, Marvin in 1956, and Dorothy in 1959. Tragedy struck in 1953 when Robin died of **leukemia**.

Bush graduated from college in three years. In 1948, Bush got a job offer from his father's investment firm. But he turned it down. Bush wanted to make his own way through life.

Bush moved his family to Texas. There, he took a job sweeping warehouses and painting oil well parts. Bush learned the oil business quickly. He became a supply salesman for Dresser Industries.

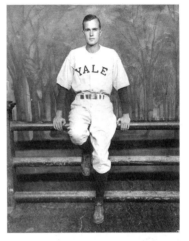

Bush in his Yale uniform

Barbara and George with their first child

Successful Businessman

*I*n 1951, George Bush and John Overbey became business partners. They started the Bush-Overbey Oil Development Company in Midland, Texas. They bought rights to drill for oil.

In 1953, Bush started another company. He called it Zapata **Petroleum** Corporation. Zapata drilled for oil. A year later, Bush formed the Zapata Off-Shore Company. It made drilling equipment. By now, Bush was rich.

Bush became interested in politics. His father had been a U.S. senator from 1952 to 1963. Bush decided to run for the Senate in 1964.

Bush was a **Republican**. But most Texans were **Democrats**. They didn't think he would win the election. Bush ran a strong campaign. People liked his ideas. He lost the election, but it was a close race.

In 1966, Bush quit the oil business to work in politics. He ran for the U.S. **House of Representatives** and won. Now, he was the first Republican to represent Houston in **Congress**.

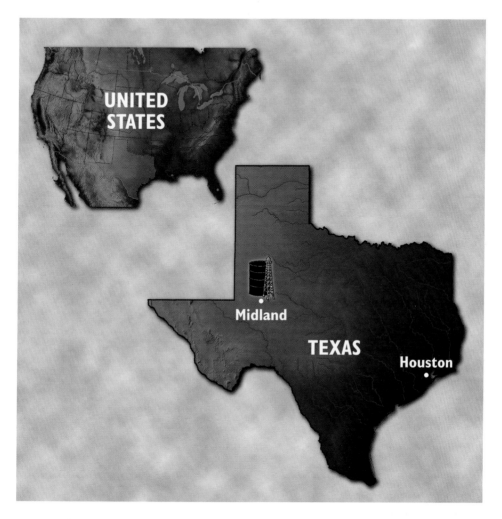

Bush supported laws that would lower the voting age to 18 and end the military **draft**. In 1970, Bush ran for the U.S. Senate, but lost the election. Bush was upset. He wanted to stay in politics.

The Making of the Forty-first United States President

1924
Born June 12 in Milton, Massachusetts

1942
Graduates from Phillips Academy

1942
Joins the U.S. Navy

1943
Assigned to a torpedo bomber squadron

1948
Graduates from Yale University

1951
Helps start the Bush-Overbey Oil Development Company

1953
Starts the Zapata Petroleum Corporation

1964
Runs for the U.S. Senate, but loses the election

1974
Named first U.S. envoy to the People's Republic of China

1976
Heads the Central Intelligence Agency (CIA)

1980
Elected U.S. vice president

1984
Re-elected U.S. vice president

George Bush

"We as a people have such a purpose today. It is to make kinder the face of the nation and gentler the face of the world."

1945 → **1945** → **1946**

Marries Barbara Pierce on January 6

Enters Yale University

First child, George W., is born

Historic Events
during Bush's Presidency

★ Hubble Space Telescope launched

★ Bush signs Civil Rights Act of 1991

★ Los Angeles, California, erupts in race riots

1966 → **1971** → **1973**

Elected to the House of Representatives

Appointed U.S. ambassador to the United Nations

Becomes chairman of the Republican National Committee

1988

Elected U.S. president

1991

Persian Gulf War

1992

Defeated by Bill Clinton in election for president

PRESIDENTIAL YEARS

Working in Politics

*P*resident Richard Nixon chose Bush to be the U.S. **ambassador** to the **United Nations** in 1971. Bush worked closely with other countries. He helped them with their problems.

The **Watergate Scandal** erupted in 1973. Bush became the head of the **Republican National Committee**. He led the **Republican** party through this difficult time. A year later, Bush urged Nixon to leave the White House.

In 1974, Vice President Gerald Ford became president. Ford made Bush the U.S. **envoy** to the People's Republic of China. Bush strengthened ties between the two nations. He returned home in 1975.

Richard Nixon

In 1976, Bush became head of the **Central Intelligence Agency (CIA)**. He improved the agency's ability to gather information about other countries.

Bush wanted to be the U.S. president. In 1977, he worked on his campaign for the 1980 election.

Ronald Reagan won the election. He asked Bush to be his vice president. Bush was now one step away from the White House.

Bush (left) advises Vice President Gerald Ford during the Watergate Scandal in 1973.

The Forty-first President

Vice President Bush led many political groups. He visited more than 70 countries. He also helped plan America's fight against drugs and **terrorism**.

In 1988, Americans had to elect a new president. By law, Reagan could not be president after two terms. So, **Republicans** chose Bush to run. Bush picked J. Danforth "Dan" Quayle to be his vice president.

In the election, Bush defeated **Democrat** Michael Dukakis. Bush became the nation's forty-first president on January 20, 1989.

America had trouble with Panama. Manuel Noriega was its leader. He sent drugs into the United States. In 1989, he said Panama and America were at war.

Manuel Noriega

18

Bush acted quickly. In December, he sent soldiers to Panama. Noriega got away, but gave up on January 3, 1990. U.S. soldiers brought him to America to stand trial. Noriega went to jail for selling drugs.

Bush had promised the nation that he would not raise taxes. But in June 1990, Bush could not keep that promise. Money was needed to pay for government programs. Americans were upset with the tax increase.

President Bush was good at solving problems with other countries. This helped him be a leader in world affairs. In 1991, he signed a treaty with Russia. It reduced the number of nuclear weapons in both countries.

The Seven "Hats" of the U.S. President

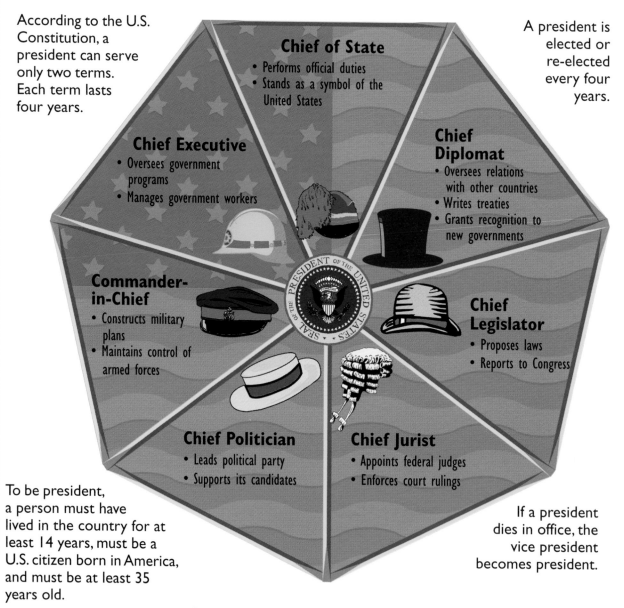

According to the U.S. Constitution, a president can serve only two terms. Each term lasts four years.

A president is elected or re-elected every four years.

Chief of State
- Performs official duties
- Stands as a symbol of the United States

Chief Executive
- Oversees government programs
- Manages government workers

Chief Diplomat
- Oversees relations with other countries
- Writes treaties
- Grants recognition to new governments

Commander-in-Chief
- Constructs military plans
- Maintains control of armed forces

Chief Legislator
- Proposes laws
- Reports to Congress

Chief Politician
- Leads political party
- Supports its candidates

Chief Jurist
- Appoints federal judges
- Enforces court rulings

PRESIDENT OF THE UNITED STATES · SEAL OF THE

To be president, a person must have lived in the country for at least 14 years, must be a U.S. citizen born in America, and must be at least 35 years old.

If a president dies in office, the vice president becomes president.

As president, George Bush had seven jobs.

The Three Branches of the U.S. Government

Congress is in the Capitol Building in Washington, D.C. It can pass laws and stop the president's veto. Congress also can change the Constitution to stop the president's plans or Supreme Court rulings.

The president lives in the White House in Washington, D.C. He or she can stop (veto) laws passed by Congress, and propose new laws. The president also can choose Supreme Court judges.

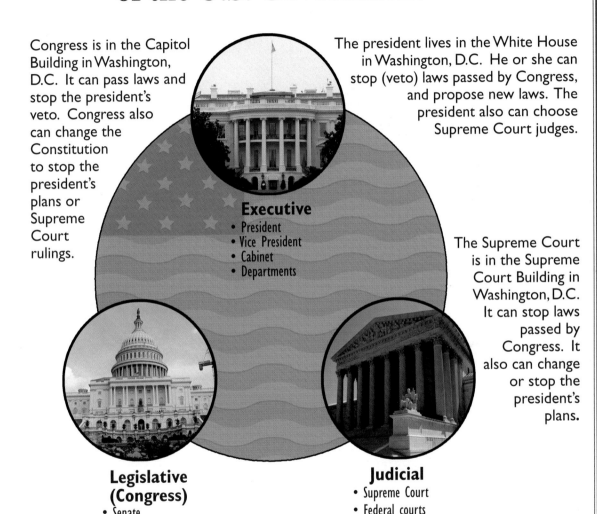

Executive
- President
- Vice President
- Cabinet
- Departments

The Supreme Court is in the Supreme Court Building in Washington, D.C. It can stop laws passed by Congress. It also can change or stop the president's plans.

Legislative (Congress)
- Senate
- House of Representatives

Judicial
- Supreme Court
- Federal courts

The U.S. Constitution formed three government branches. Each branch has power over the others. So, no single group or person can control the country. The Constitution calls this "separation of powers."

War in the Gulf

*B*ush also showed strong leadership during the Persian Gulf War.

Saddam Hussein was the leader of Iraq. Iraq owed other nations 50 million dollars. Hussein wanted Kuwait's oil. He could sell it to pay back the money. So, Iraq attacked Kuwait in August 1990. Hussein claimed that Kuwait was part of Iraq.

World leaders tried to get Iraq to leave Kuwait. They feared Iraq would invade other Middle East countries and claim their oil. But Hussein refused to withdraw his troops.

As commander-in-chief, President Bush acted swiftly. He got other countries to act as **allies** against Iraq. And he sent thousands of troops to protect Saudi Arabia from invasion. This military action was called Operation Desert Shield.

Saddam Hussein

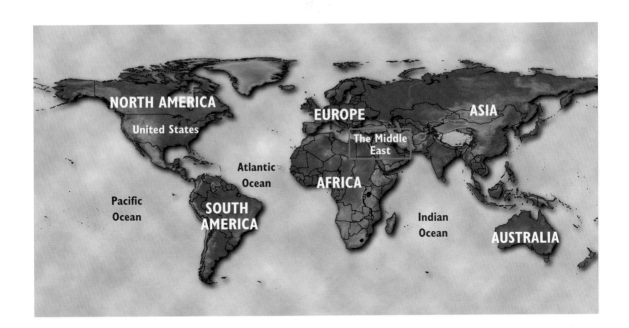

NORTH AMERICA

United States

EUROPE

ASIA

The Middle
East

Atlantic
Ocean

AFRICA

Pacific
Ocean

SOUTH
AMERICA

Indian
Ocean

AUSTRALIA

THE MIDDLE EAST

MEDITERRANEAN SEA

Iraq

Kuwait

AFRICA

Saudi
Arabia

PERSIAN
GULF

RED
SEA

America and its **allies** demanded that Iraq leave Kuwait. Still, the Iraqis did not go.

The Persian Gulf War began on January 16, 1991. America and its allies bombed Iraq from airplanes. They blew up bridges, highways, and airports. The attack was called Operation Desert Storm.

In January, the Iraqis released oil into the Persian Gulf. They set oil wells on fire. The spilled oil killed animals, fish, and birds. Smoke from the fires caused air pollution and acid rain.

Allied soldiers attacked Iraq on February 23. The fighting lasted only four days. Iraq's soldiers gave up. The Persian Gulf War ended February 27.

An oil field worker prays near a burning oil well in Kuwait.

24

"It is a time of pride, pride in our troops, pride in our friends who stood by us during the crisis, and pride in our great nation," Bush told America. His re-election seemed certain.

But in 1992, the U.S. economy was in trouble. Prices for goods were high. Jobs were hard to find. People blamed Bush. He claimed the economy would soon improve.

Americans did not believe President Bush. On November 3, 1992, they elected Bill Clinton president.

George Bush with U.S. soldiers during the Persian Gulf War

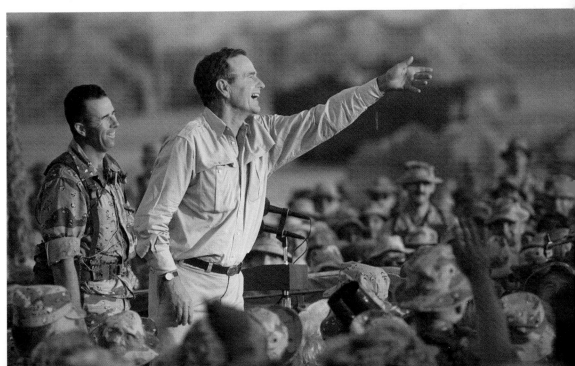

President Bush Goes Home

*A*fter George Bush left the White House, he continued to give back to his country. He visited China and Vietnam to improve relations. In 1997, the U.S. government had more problems with Iraq. They asked Bush for advice.

George and Barbara continue to help others with **volunteer** work. They support the study of **leukemia**. And they help people learn how to read and write.

The Bushes also support the President's Summit for America's Future, and the Points of Light Foundation. These groups encourage Americans to do volunteer community service, and help solve social problems.

Barbara Bush reads a story to grade school students in Mesa, Arizona.

In 1997, the George Bush Presidential Library in College Station, Texas, was completed. Former presidents, family, and friends attended the opening.

George and Barbara love to spend time with their family. Their children, grandchildren, and nieces and nephews are their biggest pride and joy.

George Bush has had a remarkable life. He was a **World War II** pilot, Yale graduate, and successful businessman. He became a congressman, **envoy**, and vice president. As president, Bush will be remembered for his strong leadership during the Persian Gulf War.

The George Bush Presidential Library

Fun Facts

- On March 25, 1997, at the age of 72, George Bush joined members of the U.S. Golden Knight precision parachute team and jumped out of an airplane and parachuted to the ground.

- First baseman George Bush was the captain of his Yale baseball team. He was presented with the original manuscript of the *Babe Ruth Story* by baseball legend Babe Ruth. The manuscript is in the Yale Library.

- George Bush has two sons in politics. Jeb Bush is the governor of Florida. George W. Bush is the governor of Texas.

- Bush's grandfather, G. H. Walker, was an excellent golfer. Walker started a competition for golfers in 1923. He called it the Walker Cup. **Amateur** golfers from the United States and Great Britain still play for the Walker Cup every year.

*Babe Ruth (left) presents to Yale baseball captain George Bush the original manuscript of the **Babe Ruth Story**. This photo was taken at Yale Field, New Haven, Connecticut, in 1948.*

Glossary

allies - countries that agree to help each other in times of need.

amateur - someone who does not play for money.

ambassador - a representative sent from one government to meet with another.

Central Intelligence Agency (CIA) - part of the U.S. government that gathers information about other countries.

Congress - the lawmaking body of a nation. It is made up of the Senate and the House of Representatives.

Democrat - one of the two main political parties in the United States. Democrats are often liberal and believe in more government.

draft - a method of choosing people for service in the military.

envoy - a representative from a government, below an ambassador.

House of Representatives - a group of people elected by citizens to represent them. They meet in Washington, D.C., and make laws for the country.

leukemia - a blood disease.

peninsula - a piece of land almost surrounded by water.

petroleum - a liquid (also called oil) from wells drilled in the ground. It is used to make gasoline, fuel oils, and other products.

Republican - one of two main political parties in the United States. Republicans are often conservative and believe in less government.

Republican National Committee - the group of people who run the Republican party.

terrorism - the use of violence to threaten people or governments.

United Nations - a worldwide group formed in 1945 to promote peace.

volunteer - to offer help.

Watergate Scandal - a 1972 political crime involving President Nixon and his administration. Nixon's people broke into the Watergate Building and tried to steal information about the Democrats. The burglars were caught and sent to jail. Nixon was forced to quit.

World War II - 1939-1945. The U.S., Great Britain, France, the Soviet Union, and their allies fought Germany, Italy, Japan, and their allies.

Internet Sites

George Bush Presidential Library and Museum
http://bushlibrary.tamu.edu/
Visit the official Web site of the 41st president, George Bush. This site has an extensive biography on President Bush along with his speeches, cabinet, photos, and a kid's page.

Welcome to the White House
http://www.whitehouse.gov
The official Web site of the White House has an introduction from the United State's current president. Also included is extensive biographies of each president, White House history information, art in the White House, First Ladies, and First Families. Visit the section titled: The White House for Kids, where kids can become more active in the government of the United States.

POTUS—Presidents of the United States
http://www.ipl.org/ref/POTUS/
In this Web site you will find background information, election results, cabinet members, presidency highlights, and some odd facts on each of the presidents. Links to biographies, historical documents, audio and video files, and other presidential sites are also included to enrich this site.

These sites are subject to change. Go to your favorite search engine and type in United States presidents for more sites.

Pass It On

History enthusiasts: educate readers around the country by passing on information you've learned about presidents or other important people who have changed history. Share your little-known facts and interesting stories. We want to hear from you!

To get posted on the ABDO Publishing Company Web site, email us at "History@abdopub.com"
Visit the ABDO Publishing Company Web site at www.abdopub.com

Index